Outsourced Freelancing Success

How to Set Freelancing Rates and Get Paid What You're Worth!

Lise Cartwright

Part of the OFS Guide Book Series

Published by

www.vixenink.com

Cover Design by Steve Windsor

www.outsourcedfreelancingsuccess.com
For queries, please email: lise@outsourcedfreelancingsuccess.com

Get Your Freebie!

STOP!

Before you go any further, don't forget to pick up your free gifts!

As a thank you for buying this book, I'd love to give you access to my
Email Pitch Template that I use to approach clients directly about jobs, as well as a copy of my **Proposal Template (+ example)** that I use when applying for jobs on outsourcing sites (can be adapted to work for larger pitches to clients too!).

On top of that, you'll also get access to my PDF report on the **10 Mistakes New Freelancers Make (AND How You Can Avoid Them).**

Go to: www.outsourcedfreelancingsuccess.com/10-mistakes-sign-up **now!**

Dedication

To all my loyal OFS Newsletter Subscribers, for sticking with me and sharing in the journey—you guys rock!

:: Table of Contents

THE ISSUE IN A NUTSHELL

One of the hardest things to figure out when you first start freelancing is what to charge.

It's one of the most commonly asked questions I get from the Outsourced Freelancing Success blog, and one that a lot of people are just plain confused about.

And that's understandable—particularly if you've never had to think about how much to charge for a specific project or skill set, nor have you ever had to do this in your current job.

There is a lot of negative "stigma" around freelancing, in that prospective clients may feel that they should be getting access to your skills at a lower rate than what they might pay a full-time employee.

This is definitely not the case, and if your skill is in a very specific niche, you will be paid very well depending on your skill set.

If you're working in a role where you have to provide quotes for jobs all the time, then you'll find working out your freelancing rate a little easier. However, there are a few things that go into your freelancing rate—things that you might not have thought of...

I know when I first started freelancing, I was paralyzed by fear initially. I'd never had to price my work before, nor had I really had to consider things like overheads or how much my time was actually worth, which made working out my rate quite difficult and more than a little intimidating the first time round.

I was also worried that my price might not be what the client was expecting, or that I was going to completely undervalue my skills or the project scope and be stuck with that rate forever.

It took me a while to figure out how to set my rate, mainly through a lot of trial and error...

If you're not familiar with my story, I started out freelancing on the side using oDesk.

I can remember one of my first SEO writing jobs

paying me a piddly $10 for a 500 word article—but at the time, I didn't have any ratings on oDesk, so no one was willing to pay me what I was asking for (or what I deserved).

Once I'd completed a few jobs on oDesk, it became increasingly clear to me that if I was going to make a living as a freelancer, I'd have to raise my rates accordingly, and fast!

One of the hardest things I found was figuring out what the work I was doing was valued at compared with the amount of time it actually took me to complete said work, and then what the value was on MY actual time.

After completing a few jobs on oDesk and getting some good ratings, I sat down and came up with a formula to work out how much I should charge per project, or per hour, as the case may be.

I'm going to share that formula with you, so that you can figure this out for yourself too.

I wrote this book as a guide to help you navigate your way through determining what your freelancing rate is, how to price per project, and then how to negotiate your rates and really get paid what you're worth.

:: How This Guide Works

This guide is split into four main sections as follows:

- Section 1: *Understanding Your Market (aka Your Skillset)*

- Section 2: *Working Out Your Rate*

- Section 3: *Negotiating Rates*

- Section 4: *Best Practices*

At the end of this book, you'll find links to resources and tools to help you with this process as well.

Before we can work out your rate, we need to look at your specific market and make sure that you take a few things into consideration first.

Once you understand your market and the demand for your skills, then we can move on and look at how to work out your rate.

Let's jump straight into it. Turn the page to find out more about your market and, in particular, what you need to know before you can set your rate and get paid what you're worth.

SECTION 1: UNDERSTANDING YOUR MARKET (AKA YOUR SKILLSET)

Your Skillset

Before you can really work out your freelancing rate, you need to understand your specific market and customer needs.

Your market is split into three areas:

1. What your potential client/customer wants

2. What the demand is for your skill

3. What is the average fee charged?

Let's look at these areas in more detail, so that we can better understand them and use them to help figure out our initial freelancing rate.

:: Client/Customer Needs

A lot of freelancers fail to do this when they are just starting out. They fail to think about what their potential clients or customers are actually looking for.

Instead, they make assumptions, which can quickly lead to your freelancing business failing or experiencing a dry spell for a long period of time.

To avoid this happening to you, ask yourself these questions:

1. What's important to your potential client?

2. Are they looking for speed? Efficiency? Beauty? Accuracy? Simplicity? Affordability?

3. What order do these requests go in?

You can get this type of information by first reviewing jobs requests on sites like oDesk.com or Elance.com. In most instances, the client is very specific about what they're looking for.

Take note of what some of the more common themes are as they relate to your skills.

Keep these close by for further on in the chapter.

:: Demand for Your Skill

This is something that you should probably have looked at already, and definitely something you should review before you quit your day job—what is the demand level for your specific skillset?

Again, the easiest way to determine this is to look at sites like oDesk and Elance and see how many jobs are being posted in your category.

From there, you'll wanna look at how many people have applied for that role in the space of an hour (generally the last hour).

If you can find pages and pages of jobs for your skill, that's a great sign. But before you jump for joy, there is another factor that determines the demand for your skill.

What is it?

The number of freelancers with the same skillset as you.

Going back to oDesk or Elance, look at those same jobs you looked at before and see how many free-lancers have applied for those roles within the last hour.

If it's more than 20, then that particular skill may be in high demand, but the overall market de-mand is low because there are a lot of freelancers servicing that skill.

If you were to find less than 10 freelancers apply-ing for a job within the last hour, then the demand for your skill is higher and this means you can charge accordingly.

:: **Average Fee**

Once you've figured out the demand for your skill set, it's time to figure out what the average fee is being charged for the skills you'd like to focus on for your freelancing business.

Again, viewing oDesk or Elance, see if you can find jobs that have been completed and what amount the client was willing to pay.

Split this information into hourly versus fixed fees and you'll get a good idea what the average charge is for your particular skill set.

Another consideration when it comes to fees is: What are new freelancers charging compared with more experienced ones? You can view free-lancers on either oDesk or Elance and view what they are charging by looking at their profile.

You can tell if they're new by the date they joined.

Once you've got all of this information together, you can move onto the next section and work out your rates.

Now it's time for you to actually DO something. Part of being a successful freelancer includes not just reading, but doing.

Below you'll find some action items to help you understand what you've just read, as well as keep track of your progress.

:: Take Action! Checklist

- Do some research and figure out what your client's actual needs are. Do this for each project/gig you apply for.

- Determine what the demand is for your skillset by reviewing the number of jobs available versus the number of freelancers applying.

- Determine what the average fee is for the jobs you're looking to apply for. Look at both new freelancers and more established ones to determine the average charge.

Where do You Fit?

Once you've done a bit of research and know what the market is like for your skillset, it's time to figure out where your rate will fit in amongst all of that.

One of the best ways to do this is to take stock of where you would class your skill level at for your particular freelancing niche.

Are you experienced because this niche is something that you participate in as part of your current day job? Or are you maybe intermediate in your skill, meaning that you don't quite have all the qualifications you need to be classed as a senior or experienced person in your particular industry?

You'll probably already have a fairly good idea of where you fit, but if you're really not sure, one of the quickest ways to figure this out would be to do some of the tests on oDesk or Elance as they relate to your specific skill set.

For example, say you were a graphic designer, you could take tests that would confirm your level of expertise about that skill, while also proving that you know what you're doing to prospective clients.

I'd recommend that you do these tests regardless of where you believe you fit. They will confirm what you already know, and if they don't, i.e., you fail or score below average on a test, you'll know which skills or areas you'll need to brush up on.

:: Working Directly With Clients

If you're planning to work directly with clients, rather than start out with outsourcing sites, the above exercise is even more important.

Another key factor in working out your rate when working with clients directly is what you've got set up in your portfolio (you have one, right?!).

Your portfolio is like your *online business card*, so make sure you've got it current and looking good, and if you don't have anything to put in it as yet, create a few items so that you have something to show a potential client.

Using the email pitch template that you were given at the beginning of this book is ideal for use with direct clients.

In most instances, if you're working directly with a client, you probably already know their budget or what they are willing to pay for this particular role.

If you do know the proposed payment amount already, make sure it aligns with your freelancing rate and then adjust accordingly.

You'll learn more about how to negotiate rates in *Section 3*, but for now, figure out where you fit as a freelancer compared to your peers in your niche and then move on to *Section 2: Working Out Your Rate.*

SECTION 2: WORKING OUT YOUR RATE

The Formula

Now we've come to the most exciting part of the book—figuring out how much you should (or could) be charging for roles in your niche.

When I first started out freelancing, I remember thinking that my current hourly rate at my day job would be a good place to start—how wrong I was...

As I mentioned previously, if you've never had to work out specific costs for a job before, it can be really overwhelming and more than a little confusing, and if you get it wrong, it could mean losing a potential client.

NOT what you wanna have happen anytime soon!

Add to this the layer that quite often, the skill

you're freelancing with is not easily definable, making it even harder to figure out a rate.

:: Things to Consider When Setting Your Rate

Before we jump into the formula, here is a closer look at some of the things that go into building the formula.

Make sure you know your response to each of these individual things ahead of time, where possible, so you can work out your rate for specific projects.

Length of time it takes to complete a task:
Whether you opt to go with an hourly rate or not, you need to know how long it's going to take you to complete each task associated with a project. In most cases, this is going to be a guesstimate. We'll talk about this more, but working out what your hourly rate is provides a good baseline to start with when pricing projects for a client. I wouldn't advise you to tell your client what your hourly rate is, as that can lead to a very big rabbit hole that can be difficult to extricate yourself from.

Always quote a project fee only.

Project costs: Do you need to buy supplies or software to complete this project? You might have to buy photos or domain names, so make sure that these are factored into any project fees you quote.

Your overheads: This is things like your internet connection, power usage, rent or mortgage, marketing, insurance, etc. Know what these are for a 12 month period and then work out what portion of this will need to be added to your project fee. This is particularly important if you're going to be working on a project for longer than a month.

Profit: This is a percentage that you'll add once you've figured everything else out. It reflects your experience and the value you bring to the project.

Market conditions: This is something you will need to factor in; particularly when there's a lot of demand for your work, you can charge slightly higher rates. If there isn't a lot of demand, then you'll need to price your rates accordingly. It's all about perceived value and demand from your clients perspective.

Tax: You're going to have to pay tax at some point, so factoring this in now is your best bet to ensure that you don't get landed with any unexpected tax bills. Consult a local accountant on what tax you'll be liable for. If you're still working full-time, you will more than likely offset any tax by claiming expenses on your taxable income, but a qualified accountant will give you the best advice on this. I'm no tax specialist!

:: How to Calculate Your Rate

The first area of the formula is focused on determining your base rate, which is often referred to as your hourly rate or minimum acceptable rate (MAR).

This is what I use to determine my base rate initially:

Average Hours Worked per Month (x minimum wage + 10%) + Monthly Overheads/Average Hours

Worked = Hourly Rate

Once you work out this amount, you could use this as your bottom line or MAR. This would be the minimum I would accept for a job, regardless of whether it was hourly or fixed.

Once you've identified your base rate, you need to work out the rest of your project rate using this formula:

Base Rate x Approx. Hours to Complete Project + Project Costs + Profit % + Tax = Project fee

Once you've got these two formulas ready, it's time to apply it to some actual jobs. On the next page you'll learn how to actually work out a fee based on different project specifications. Turn the page to find out more...

Working Out a Fee

Ok, now that you've got the formula, it's time to look at how this works in practice.

:: Starting With Outsourcing Sites

If you plan to start freelancing by accessing roles on sites like oDesk or Elance, your initial first few jobs are going to need to reflect your inexperience on these platforms. I know that probably sounds counter-intuitive, but there is a reason for my madness...

It might annoy you that you have to charge yourself out at a low rate for the first couple, but it's the only way to get started on these sites.

Ratings matter—they are the currency of outsourcing sites and without one, it's difficult to charge higher rates or access the better jobs. At least initially anyway.

Keep this in mind as you're putting forward proposals for the first time.

My advise to you and to my coaching clients is that your aim should be to get 3-5 jobs as quickly as possible, aiming for quick turnaround jobs that pay low, just so you can get some ratings on the board.

Once you've completed these first few jobs, start to increase your rate with each new client, until you're at an hourly (or project) rate you're comfortable with, remembering that you'll need to be a little flexible. More on that in the next section, *Section 3: Negotiating Rates.*

:: **Other Sites or Working Directly With Clients**

If you decide to move off outsourcing sites and work directly with clients or work with a niche-specific site, you can set your rates at a higher price point, particularly if you have a great portfolio to back this up with.

Again, my initial advice would be to start working

on outsourcing sites first, then move to working with clients directly, either through referrals or your network after a period of 6+ months—give yourself some time to build out your portfolio.

:: Working Out Project Rates

It's important to note that your rate may vary from client-to-client, so it pays to have a way to figure out how you're going to set your rate for each project you work on, keeping in mind this could be for both hourly and fixed (project) rates.

Let's look at how this might actually work in practice, starting with your base (hourly) rate that you worked out previously.

In our example, we're going to assume you're a *part-time graphic designer*.

Using the base rate formula (*Average Hours Worked per Month (x minimum wage + 10%) + Monthly Overheads/Average Hours Worked = Hourly Rate*), we'll assume:

- Average Hours worked per month = 20 x

$55 = $1,100

- Monthly Overheads = $110

$1,100 + $110 / 20 = $60.00 is your hourly rate

Taking this as our MAR amount, we can then work out a project fee, for both hourly and fixed, as needed.

In this example, the job you're applying for is to provide the client with a new logo in three different formats, as well as a banner for their website. You've been assigned four days in which to deliver the project.

Here's how we'd work out the project fee (*Base Rate x Approx. Hours to Complete Project + Project Costs + Profit % + Tax = Project fee*):

$60 x 5 hours + $100 (images) + 15% + 30% (Tax) = $598.00

Another option is to price per service rather than by hours worked.

Using a different example this time; as a freelance writer, I would normally charge per blog post or article, rather than using a base rate to determine my project fee.

Let's use the same example with relation to the profit and tax amounts, and see what this looks like based on 10 x 550 word blog posts at a rate of $35 per post:

$35 x 10 blog posts + 0 + 15% + 30% = $523.25

Depending on the type of services you're providing as a freelancer, this might be a better option.

You could also work out your hourly rate, if the client prefers to use this, by taking your base rate and adding the profit amount and tax amount to it, this way you ensure you're getting paid a fair amount and covering your tax obligations. This would be my recommendation for working our your MAR.

Let's look at a final example of how this might look. For this example, you're a freelance copy-writer.

You've worked out that your base rate is $55 per hour. For this particular gig, you've been asked to write a sales page + 20 pages of website content for a site.

The formula for this might look something like this:

$$\textit{\$55 x 7 hours + 0 + 15\% + 30\% = \$575.58}$$

The bottom line is, you don't want to undervalue your work, nor do you want to get so consumed with choosing your rate that you end up picking a number out of thin air.

It helps to have an idea of your base rate or MAR

before you even start taking on work.

I know this can be difficult to do if you haven't worked as a freelancer before, but if you're committed to getting your freelancing career off the ground, it's safe to assume you'd likely average 20 hours a month, so that's definitely where I'd recommend you start your formula at.

Just remember, if you're pricing for outsourcing sites, you might have to price lower initially, but once your credibility is proved and you have a good rating and client feedback, you can increase your rates very quickly.

:: Project Rate vs Hourly Rate

Before we move onto the next section where we're going to talk about the scary part—negotiating rates, let's talk about the differences between hourly and fixed rates (or project rate) first.

An hourly rate is where you trade your time for dollars (like you do/did as an employee), whereas a fixed or project rate allows you to price based on a number of different factors.

Either can be a good option, depending on the client and the job.

I'm not going to say I prefer one over the other, but there are definitely times when quoting an hourly rate might be to your advantage over a fixed or project rate and vice versa.

Let's look at some of the scenarios and what I'd recommend you charge.

Ongoing or Long-term Project

If you have a long-term client or role that is ongoing, charging the client an hourly rate is a far more effective use of your time and theirs.

It saves you having to continuously draw up contracts, and as long as you track your time correctly, it's an easy and fair way to charge.

Just remember to add a profit margin to your rate that reflects your experience and expertise, i.e., use your MAR.

Project Goals and Deadline are Unknown

For this type of role, you'd want to stick with an hourly rate also. The main reason I'd recommend this is because if you were to provide a fixed rate for the project, what happens when the project goes over scope and time, effectively going above what you'd priced on?

You're left out of pocket and very frustrated.

If you charge hourly, it also ensures that your client respects your time, as they can clearly see how much per hour you're charging and the number of hours you're working. It dissuades them from asking for non-essential work, because they know you're going to charge them for it.

It also provides you with the ability to push back as well or charger a higher rate if you need to turn other work away.

You Have Multiple Clients in Different Services

If you provide more than one service to clients, it's likely that you'll have a different rate for each of these services. In this case, a project rate would be to your advantage, provided this isn't ongoing work.

This is also beneficial if you're looking to increase your rate or your clients refer you to other clients. If you have an hourly rate, you could end up being pigeon-holed into that rate.

Be very clear that your fee depends on a number of factors, so that clients are aware that your hourly fee is not set in stone when recommending you to other clients.

Client is Unsure of Exact Scope

If you have a client that has no idea of the scope of a project, or they simply have no idea what you actually do for them, then a project rate is your best option.

Make sure you spell out exactly what you'll be doing for them in the contract, otherwise you could land yourself in a bit of hot water if they balk at your pricing. Be clear and transparent about what you do and you'll lower the chance of this issue arising.

Increase Your Productivity

If you're looking to increase your productivity, opt to charge per project rather than per hour. When you charge per hour, you can lapse back into trading dollars for time, which isn't ideal long-term if you want to stay engaged and interested in what you do.

Are You Fast?

Are you fast at what you do? Just because you're quick, doesn't mean you should charge a smaller fee. Aim to charge by the project if this is you. This way, you don't undervalue what it is you do, and you don't get penalized because your skills allow you to be quick.

Client is on a Strict Budget

This is quite a common occurrence, so if you're faced with someone saying that they are on a budget, price by the project rather than the hour. If you provide your hourly rate, they could get a little nervous. If they know your exact (total) fee up front, they can prepare and budget accordingly.

As you start down the road of freelancing, you'll soon realize that a combination of both fixed and hourly rates can be a good way to go. It provides you with flexibility and allows you to control how you're paid for what you do.

On the next page, you'll find the action steps for this section. Don't skip over these—setting your rate is one of the most important aspects of being successful as a freelancer!

Now it's time for you to actually DO something. Part of being a successful freelancer includes not just reading, but doing.

Below you'll find some action items to help you understand what you've just read, as well as help keep track of your progress.

:: Take Action Checklist

- Work out your base rate.

- Find some jobs you could apply for and try working out a project fee and an hourly fee.

- Apply for some gigs with your new rate, whether fixed or hourly.

SECTION 3: NEGOTIATING RATES

Now that you've worked out what your potential fees are going to be, it's time to brush up on your negotiating skills. How well you can negotiate going forward, will directly determine how well your freelancing business blossoms or dies a horrible death!

The reason for this is that there is a lot of room for movement when chatting with a client about a potential job. They will always ask for your "*best*" *price*, but you should also keep in mind that they have a bit of room to move too.

Enter the negotiations...

Now I know what you're thinking. You're thinking to yourself, "Geese, Lise, I hate negotiating. I just wanna get paid what I'm worth..."

Well, if you wanna get paid what you're worth,

you need to be able to negotiate; it's plain and simple.

But it doesn't have to be difficult...

Once you know what your minimum acceptable rate (MAR) is (the least amount you'll accept on any job), from there, once you know how to work out your fee on any project, negotiating a fair rate is easy.

:: Negotiating The Right Way

Negotiating wasn't something that came naturally to me. Prior to going freelancing, I'd never been in a position where I'd had to really negotiate anything, at least not something that I really cared about or that mattered.

When I was faced with my first client outside of oDesk, I was forced to negotiate, particularly because the client was grossly underestimating the scope of the project we were going to be working on, and because I didn't want to be undervalued.

In essence, I had to put my big girl pants on and

figure this stuff out!

And don't get me wrong, most clients that you work with are not after a cheap deal at all, they are just looking for the best price and to save money where they can, just like any business.

Once you understand that, it does make the negotiating process a lot easier to handle.

Follow these steps to ensure that your negotiations go the right way:

Make sure that you understand the scope of the job. You can't price a job unless you're fully aware of what's required of you and the length of time it'll take. A big mistake new freelancers make is in this very aspect.

Ask questions, and make sure you have everything you need to know about the job before you even talk about providing a quote.

As you begin the process of pricing the job, make sure you know what all the components are that make up the job. Use the formula from the previous section to work out your starting fee. Once you've done that, if the job is a long one or it is happening in various stages, make sure that you allow for this.

In this instance, you'd want to price the job out in terms of each stage and then add a buffer on top of that.

Side Note: If this is a new client, they are more likely to negotiate than not, so be prepared for this (negotiating your price) to happen.

A client could feel hard done by if they are not provided with a price that has had a little taken off it, so factor this into your pricing. What do I mean by this? Always price at the higher end initially, so that that when the client comes back to you, you can knock off 10-15 % and not be selling yourself short.

Negotiating With Existing Clients

Personally, I find negotiating with new clients far easier than with existing. The main reason for this? Existing clients tend to have an expectation that *"you'll look after them,"* which often translates into expecting discounting work that can lead to going below your base rate, or MAR.

You really only have three options when this happens:

1. Accept what they are proposing.

2. Stand your ground on the fee you've put forward.

3. Negotiate with different parts of the work.

With Option 1, you should only consider this if you feel that the indirect benefits you'll receive far outweigh the difference between what you'll actually receive compared to your base rate.

For example, I have a long-term client that provides consistent, ongoing work. He refers all his clients to me for copywriting work, so I charge him a little below my base rate.

I'm okay with this because of the benefit I receive from working with him.

Keep this in mind when negotiating with any client.

With Option 2, stand your ground if you feel that your MAR is fair and reasonable for the work being requested and there are no indirect benefits to you in taking a lower price.

Be prepared to lose a potential client when you have to take this route, but in reality, you're far better to do this than take on work outside of your minimum acceptable rate for nothing in return.

Option 3, is probably my least favorite of the three. You could end up compromising on service delivery, which can lead to client dissatisfaction and a client-freelancer relationship that isn't functional long-term.

There are not many circumstances that would call for Option 3, so tread carefully if you have a client that asks you to change the way that you deliver the work and in a tight timeframe—if it does feel 'right' don't agree to it.

In most instances, Option 1 or 2 should work. And

keep in mind, if a client is not prepared to accept either of these options, then why would you wanna work with them or continue to work with them anyway?

Remember, you are just as important as the client. Being a freelancer allows you the flexibility to do what you want, so don't compromise on your rates in a way that makes you wish you hadn't accepted the job...

:: A Word on Upfront Payments

As a new freelancer, you should always request a percentage of your fee upfront, particularly if you're working directly with a new client. It's for your own protection and is standard practice in the freelancing world.

This is for both working with a client on an outsourcing site or directly; it doesn't make a difference.

The only time you might not do this is if you enter

into a long-term agreement with a client and they are going to pay you a monthly retainer.

On an outsourcing site, you can request an amount up front as part of your terms. I typically aim for 30-50% upfront, depending on the scope of the project and whether I need to turn other client work away or rearrange my schedule to accommodate this client's work.

30% is perfectly normal and is something you should include in your terms.

Negotiation is about setting (and getting) terms that you are both comfortable with and can agree upon, while also remaining flexible enough to make adjustments.

Negotiating will become much easier the more clients you work with, and as long as you know what your minimum acceptable rate is, then you shouldn't ever have to worry about issues with negotiations coming up.

Now it's time for you to actually DO something. Part of being a successful freelancer includes not just reading, but doing.

Below you'll find some action items to help you understand what you've just read as well as help keep track of your progress.

:: Take Action Checklist

- Know ahead of time what your base rate or "minimum acceptable rate" is BEFORE you price a job.

- Understand that negotiating is normal and that you always have options and don't have to accept a rate if you don't want to.

- Work out what amount or percentage you'll accept for an upfront payment and in what situation you'll waive this.

Now that you can negotiate yourself into and out of a sticky situation with a client, it's time to learn some best practices as they relate to your rates.

Turn the next page to learn what these are and how you can ensure that you never miss a beat when working with a new or existing client.

SECTION 4: BEST PRACTICES

Congratulations! You should now have a very clear understanding on how to set your rates as a freelancer and how to ensure that you always get paid what you're worth (aka negotiating!).

If you're not, then head back to the formula section (*Section 2*), and make sure that you understand the mechanics of the formula and practice how you would price a number of different jobs in your specific skill base.

It's the best way to get a better understanding around setting rates and will get you more comfy with being able to provide a quote to a client quickly.

In this section, we're going to focus on best practices—best practices around setting boundaries with your clients, particularly as they relate to your rates. We're also going to chat about deadlines and contracts, two areas that can greatly affect your rate and are often forgotten once a project starts.

So turn the page to get started.

First up, we're going to talk about boundaries, because this is an area that a lot of new free-lancers can forget to put in place in the beginning, myself included!

Boundaries

As a new freelancer, it can be super exciting stepping out and doing something different, particularly if you've never worked for yourself (or from home) before.

It's like starting a new job, but even better, because you don't have any annoying bosses telling you what to do, or gossipy, long-term employees asking you pointed and intrusive questions, and you don't have to be at work at a specific time.

There is no denying that freelancing has a lot of perks. But there are some downsides, particularly if you don't think about things and prepare before taking the plunge and going full-time.

So let's talk about boundaries.

I get it, really I do. You wanna be there for the clients you have and you want them to feel special, so you go above and beyond for them. You do this because you wanna be seen as invaluable to them, so that they'll be a long-term client.

Does this seem a little needy to you?! It does to me…

When I first started freelancing full-time, I made a very serious mistake of answering my emails over the weekend. It started out as just the odd response here and there, until it was more of a Saturday morning, then all day Saturday thing.

My now husband was not overly impressed when this eventuated and it was actually he that said to me, "*Lise, are you charging more for working on the weekends? No? Then why the hell are you working right now? Can't it wait till Monday?*"

Uh-oh… I'd turned into THAT person. You know the one, constantly on their smartphones instead of enjoying their weekends.

The reality is, your clients will take up all your time if you let them, so you need to put some boundaries in place right from the get-go. And these can't be implied; there's no dilly-dallying around here.

You need to spell these boundaries out, preferably

in writing.

Here's how.

Think about the following questions:

1. When are you available to take calls?

2. When do you answer emails?

3. What will you give a little on?

4. What are your off-limits?

Write these down for yourself so that you know what your response is to these ahead of time. It can make communicating them a lot easier.

Once you've got that covered, it's important that each new client you work with is made aware of the following information very early on in your working relationship, preferably at the time you're getting them to sign a contract.

Availability During the Day?

What's your availability during normal working hours? Once you start freelancing full-time, you have your time back to yourself. You might choose to structure your day differently, and this needs to be communicated to your clients.

Similarly, if you're working a full-time job still and only freelancing part-time, you need to let your clients know when you're available and when you're not.

Availability During the Weekends?

A lot of clients believe that freelancers work whenever and wherever, so if you don't outline and set expectations up front, you could find yourself with a list minute task on a Friday that will see you scrambling over the weekend to deliver first thing Monday.

Think carefully about availability on the weekends. It can lead to some issues further down the track if you agree to do this.

With all of my clients, they know I'm not working over the weekend, but that I may respond to a few emails here and there if it's really urgent. I also let them know that this will incur an additional fee.

The mention of a fee generally deters most clients

from wanting to contact me on the weekend, but should they need to, they know they can, and that's only if I'm available.

Checking Emails

How often are you going to check your emails? Will you answer them as they come in or batch them? Let your clients know when you check your emails, otherwise you could end up with a few disgruntled clients with the expectation that you'll answer immediately.

Let them know how they can get in touch with you outside of these times, if it's urgent of course.

Checking In

This ties in nicely to the next section around deadlines, but figuring out how often you'll check in with clients is essential to receiving ongoing business from them.

Work out a system that works best for you, and let your client know about it. If they want more or less, then they can let you know.

Regardless of what you decide on any of these

points, it's important that you set these boundaries up front and early on in your working relationship.

:: Getting Feedback and Approvals

In my experience, you'll have to guide clients a lot
when it comes to providing feedback and ap-
provals on your work. For some reason, working
with a freelancer seems to provide confusion (on
the clients front) as to what we need to move
forward with on a project.

In my experience, the best way around this is to
simply tell the clients what you've done in the
past. For example, you could say something like, "*I
like to get feedback at certain points along the
project, which has worked well for me in the past. If
you could provide feedback at [here, here and
here], I think that would work well here too.*"

Make sure you clarify what type of feedback
you're looking for. If you need feedback in order
to move on, then really you're seeking their ap-

proval that you're on the right track.

It's at this point that you should also make it clear how the client can let you know that they don't like something. For example, if you were returning an article you'd written or a logo you'd designed, you could ask the client specific questions (for their comment), such as: *"Have I got the tone of this article right?"* or *"Do you like the blue I've used, or would you like something different? What about the font?"*

By being clear on how you want the feedback delivered and when, you'll ensure that you're both on the same page and avoid confusion and, potentially, multiple revision requests.

:: Revisions

On revisions, it's important that you spell out to the client how many revisions you'll provide free of charge, or that are included with your fee. The standard is 1-2 revisions and then outside of that, an additional fee is payable.

Always stipulate this in the contract, and with each draft you provide, remind the client where they are in the revision stage.

If you're providing them with their last free revision, be sure to let them know that anything further will cost them, providing an estimate for any additional work.

:: Respecting Client's Practices

Okay, so now we've been focusing solely on what we want and what our needs are, but it's also important that you take into consideration the boundaries and practices of your clients.

To find out what those are, ask a few pointed questions:

1. What's the best way for me to work with you?

2. Are there any policies or procedures that I need to be aware of?

3. When is the best time to speak with you or

email you?

The bottom line is—make sure that you know what your boundaries are, that these are communicated to your clients (and reminded often— email signatures work well for this), and that you respect how your client wishes to interact with you, provided what they request is fair.

Setting boundaries and communicating them right up front will ensure that you don't lose out on money, and allows your clients to make decisions based on the information you provide them.

In the next section, we're going to talk a bit more about deadlines, as missing them can cause huge problems for both you and your client. Turn the page to find out more.

Deadlines

When I first started out freelancing part-time, deadlines were a bit of an issue for me. I found it quite hard to balance my normal day job, my social life, and my freelancing gigs.

There were two key things that helped me in meeting deadlines:

1. Making sure that I got a definite timeframe and deadline from each client BEFORE starting work

2. Setting up a proper schedule and to-do list to manage deadlines

When you're chatting with a client about a job, find out their timeframe. You'll need this to work out your project fee anyway, so it shouldn't be an issue for them to provide this to you.

If the client is struggling to give you a definite answer, help them by prompting them:

- Will the project be split into stages?

- When were you hoping to have this completed?

- Do you have a buffer of time incorporated into this deadline?

- What happens if the work is delivered late?

By asking your client these questions, you can narrow down a timeframe and assign a deadline, allowing a buffer period of 24-48 hours (at your end), just in case life happens.

If a client refuses to give you a deadline, instead saying something like, "*within the week*," don't accept that. They could turn around the following day and demand the work.

Always ensure you can get at least an estimated deadline so you have something to work towards.

Once you've got your deadlines covered, you need to ensure you can meet those deadlines before accepting the job.

:: Meeting Deadlines

I've spoken about this at length in a number of my other books, namely *Side Hustle Blueprint: How to Make an Extra $1000 in 30 Days Without Leaving Your Day Job!* and the first book in this series, *Outsourced Freelancing Success: Start a Successful Freelancing Business and Make Your First Dollar Online!*

Either of those books will provide you with a detailed explanation of my process for managing deadlines.

Here's the "Cliff's Notes" Version:

Whether you're an organized person or not, you have to figure out a way to manage your client deadlines, otherwise you could quickly be without any clients to worry about at all.

There are a number of variations and options you can use to manage deadlines. The list below is not conclusive; there are many ways to do this, but these are the ones I've used in the past or I'm using now, so I've trialled and tested them.

Ultimately though, you have to find a system that works for your needs.

Here's some options to consider:

- Google Calendar—by far the simplest and easiest to use. Assign a color to your client work and always set the due date at least 24-48 hours in advance, so you never miss a deadline.

- Google Calendar + Evernote.com + Zapier.com, a great option if you have a lot of client information that you'd like to keep in one place.

- Google Calendar + Todoist.com + Trello.com, this is my preferred option and what I currently use to track project tasks and client-specific work.

Google Calendar is definitely your best option when you're just starting out. You can have unlimited calendars in different colors, which means that you can assign different clients with different colors, or assign colors based on the service you're providing.

Either way, it's important that you put something into practice, no matter how small that is.

Staying organized and on top of your to-do list is essential to the success and sustainability of your freelancing business. By being organized, you can increase your hourly rate and actually end up doing less hours of work.

In the next section, we're going to touch on contracts. No matter where you are in your freelancing career, having a contract in place is very important, particularly if you're just starting out. Turn the page to find out why!

Contracts

When you're going through the process of setting your rates, you should also keep in mind the contract part of the process.

:: Outsource Sites and Contracts

If you're applying for roles via outsourcing sites like oDesk, they essentially take care of this for you. If you're invited to interview, the client shares more details about the project with you, including timeframes and when and how you'll get paid.

This is their version of a binding contract.

If the client doesn't pay you, for whatever reason, you have the ability to contact the outsourcing site and get it sorted—this is the beauty of working with these types of sites; particularly when you're just starting out, they offer a lot of protection in this regard.

Side Note: Just a note on clients and outsourcing sites. Not all clients are created equal, so if you do choose to work with a client on an outsourcing site, make sure that they're payment verified. You can do this by reviewing their profile and looking for a "$" sign. On most sites, it should say "payment verified" or similar. If you can't confirm their funding status, walk away; it's that simple.

:: Working Directly with Clients and Contracts

If you end up working with a client directly, then you need to ensure that you have some type of contract in place, no matter what they might say in the way of promising you the job and payment details.

One of the best things about working with a client directly is that it gives you more freedom with your rate and it also allows you to charge a slightly higher price when compared with an outsourcing site, because the client doesn't have to pay any of the outsourcing site fees.

However, there can also be a major downside to working with clients directly—contracts, and enforcing them.

One of the best ways to ensure that a client doesn't skip out on you with your money is to have a contract drawn up by a qualified lawyer... which is costly.

There are a few options though, so choose one that works best for you. But always ensure you have something in place, in writing.

The contract should always outline what you've agreed to. Things like the scope of the work, delivery, timeframes and deadlines, and most importantly to you, when and how you'll be paid.

In most circumstances, an independent contractor agreement is your best option as a freelancer.

It covers most freelancing skills and allows you to adjust to suit your needs. You can find these by doing a Google search; however, you can't always be sure a qualified lawyer has written these, so be careful what you choose to use.

My preference is a site called ourdeal.com, where you can choose from a number of templates, fill in a few fields and then digitally sign the document.

Once you've entered in all the details, you sign it and send it off electronically to the client. They then sign and return it electronically and you receive a copy on your computer and *Our Deal* retains a copy against your account.

Lawyers write the contracts at *Our Deal* and they are enforceable. How enforceable really comes down to what you're prepared to do in order to get your money back.

If, like me, you work with clients from around the world, the ability to enforce a contract can seem difficult, but there are a lot of avenues open to you, should there be any issues.

I've only ever had to do this once. It involved a client not paying me $900 and instead of just wearing it, I contacted my local citizens advice bureau.

You'll probably have something similar wherever you live. They provided me with a legally drawn up letter that I could send to the client, that demanded the funds or further compensation would be sought... 21 days later, I received a check in the mail.

I've found that you can mitigate this from happening by ensuring that you're very clear with the client about requirements, and if you've got any concerns at all about the client, you can choose to either not work with them, or request a 50% upfront (non-refundable) payment to ensure they don't run away with the rest of your funds.

Once you've been freelancing for a while, you start to get a "feel" for whether a client is legit or not, and when that happens, it's far easier to "pull the rip cord," as my husband likes to say, than go to the trouble of working with them.

Remember, you don't have to work with every client that offers you work. It's your choice now; it's entirely up to you who you work with and who you don't.

:: Invoicing and Contracts

If you're just starting out, you probably don't have any fancy invoicing system set up, and you don't really need to in the beginning, but it will make your life easier further down the track if you do implement it now.

With the contracts I use in ourdeal.com, there is an area about payment that says that I, as the contractor, will invoice the client directly for work completed.

Depending on the type of project, I'll either load a recurring invoice into Freshbooks.com or set up a draft, one-off invoice for the client and then set a reminder for myself to send that off once the work is complete.

This means that I don't have to worry about fussing with manual invoices, nor do I have to worry about using Paypal, which can incur currency conversion fees.

This is a good practice to get into, as it ensures you don't miss sending the client an invoice, because believe me, they won't remind you!

I use <u>Freshbooks</u>, but <u>Nutcache.com</u> is another viable option and is completely free. Both link to <u>Paypal.com</u>, allowing clients to pay you directly into your Paypal account, and all you have to worry about is processing fees from Paypal. I look at it as the cost of doing business and if you speak to your tax specialist, you'll probably find that you can claim this expense back.

In the next section, you'll find a list of resources and tools mentioned throughout the book, plus a few extra ones that you might find useful when figuring out your freelancing rate.

Turn the page to learn more.

RESOURCES AND TOOLS

Welcome to the resources and tools page. You'll find a list of all the resources and tools mentioned throughout the book, plus more to help you navigate and determine your freelancing rate and ensuring you get paid what you're worth.

You can find these as a downloadable PDF by going here: www.outsourcedfreelancingsuccess.com/ResourcesPDF.

:: Sites Mentioned in the Book

- Outsourced Freelancing Succes Blog

- oDesk

- Elance

- Email Template

- OFS Guide—Book 1

- Side Hustle Blueprint—Book 1

- Our Deal

- Google Calendar

- Evernote

- Zapier

- Trello

- Todoist

- Paypal

- Freshbooks

- Nutcache

:: The Freelancing Formula's

Base Rate:

Average Hours Worked per Month (x minimum wage + 10%) + Monthly Overheads/Average Hours Worked = Hourly Rate

Project Rate:

*Base Rate x Approx. Hours to Complete Project +
Project Costs + Profit % + Tax = Project fee*

Project Rate + Service Fee:

*Individual Service Fee x # Requested + Project Costs
+ Profit % + Tax = Project fee*

:: Further Resources

- Bidsketch article on negotiating

- Inc.com article on negotiating

- Freelancers Union Community

- Your Rate (calculator for working out your base hourly rate)

- Client Scorecard (US Only)—ratings for companies that hire freelancers by freelancers who have worked with them

- Lise's <u>Freelancing Tips and Tricks Board</u> on Pinterest

Lise is a best selling author, blogger and sometimes-social media consultant and a self-confessed shoe fanatic, actually she's obsessed. Just ask her husband!

She has been looking for the magic in life since she was first exposed to positive, happy thoughts at the tender age of one - thanks Mum and Dad!

Lise can regularly be found at local cafes, NOT drinking coffee, but the more sophisticated and magical beverage that is a *Chai Latte*. She's also a bit of a baller, building her self-publishing empire at a crazy rate (think 7 books in 7 weeks!).

If you're looking to connect with Lise, you can stalk her on:

- Facebook: https://www.facebook.com/Books-byLise
- Twitter: http://www.twitter.com/Lisecnz
- Email: lise@outsourcedfreelancingsuccess.com

Her online home is located at OutsourcedFreelancing-Success.com.

Can you help?

Can you help? If you liked this book and it was help-ful to you, could you PRETTY PLEASE leave a review on Amazon? Simply visit: http://www.outsourced-freelancingsuccess.com/ofsbook2review to leave your review.

Reviews are really important to the success of a book—so if you like (or don't like!) what you've read, PLEASE take 2 minutes to leave your honest review—I really appreciate it.

:: Other Books by Lise Cartwright

You can access all of Lise's book via her Author Page here: http://www.outsourcedfreelancingsuccess.com/AuthorPage

OFS Guide Series

- Book 1: Outsourced Freelancing Success: Start a Successful Freelancing Business and Make Your First Dollar Online!
- **Book 2: *You're reading it!***
- Book 3: OFS Guide to Using Contracts With Clients and Protecting Your Business *(Release Date: 03 February 2015)*
- Book 4: OFS Guide to Setting Up and Structuring your Freelancing Business the Right Way *(Release Date: 10 February 2015)*
- Book 5: OFS Guide to Finding Clients Fast - The Top 57 Freelancing Job Sites for Finding High Paying Clients Now *(Release Date: 17 February 2015)*
- Book 6: 101 Tools and Apps to Help Run Your Successful Freelancing Business *(Release Date: 24 February 2015)*
- Book 7: 18 Ways to Grow Your Freelancing Business in 30 Days or Less *(Release Date: 28 February 2015)*

No Gym Needed Series

- Book 1: <u>No Gym Needed: Quick & Simple Work-outs for Gals on the Go</u>
- Book 2: <u>No Gym Needed: Quick & Simple Work-outs for Busy Guys</u>

If you're not a fan of the gym and like to get your exercise done in 30 minutes or less - these books are right up your alley!

Side Hustle Series

- Book 1: <u>Side Hustle Blueprint: How to Make an Extra $1000 in 30 Days Without Leaving Your Day Job</u>
- Book 2: <u>Side Hustle Blueprint: How to Make an Extra $1000 per month Writing eBooks!</u>

oDesk Guides

- <u>The Definitive Guide to Getting Freelance Writing Work on oDesk</u>
- <u>How to 'Pimp' Your oDesk Profile</u>

And if you want access to more books like this, sign up for Lise's **New Releases** author mailing list to get access to early notification of new book releases, discounts and freebies!

Click here to get started: www.lisecartwright.com

www.ingramcontent.com/pod-product-compliance
Lightning Source LLC
Chambersburg PA
CBHW070838180526
45168CB00002B/864